When Grief Is Raw

SONGS FOR TIMES OF SORROW AND BEREAVEMENT

John L. Bell
and
Graham Maule

GIA Publications, Inc.

Chicago

The Wild Goose is a Celtic symbol of the Holy Spirit
It is the trademark of Iona Community Publications

© 1997, Iona Community / Wild Goose Resource Group
Published and distributed in North America exclusively by GIA Publications, Inc.
ISBN: 1-57999-009-6

GIA Publications, Inc.
7404 S. Mason Ave.
Chicago, IL 60638
U.S.A.
(708) 496-3800

Contents

Introduction

Three main factors lie behind this collection of songs.

The first is the comment made some years ago by a ministerial colleague who noted that there was a dearth of material suitable to be sung at funerals and memorial services.

As often as not, the funeral director suggests that the family choose their or the deceased's favorite hymn, and inevitably either "Psalm 23" or "Abide With Me" appear on the service sheet. Recent years have seen the addition of "Thine Be the Glory" as an alternative to the former two or as a counter-attraction to "The Old Rugged Cross".

Unlike the sacraments of Baptism and Holy Communion, ceremonies surrounding death are offered by the churches to everyone, yet minimal attention has been paid to what is both accessible and representative in respect of texts and tunes for those who mourn.

The second contributory factor was our discovery of the immense range of emotion in the Psalms. When we were working on *Psalms of Patience, Protest and Praise,* we were recurrently startled by the daring honesty with which the writers could complain to, as well as praise, their Creator.

It may be that limp musical settings of these ancient texts or presumed over-familiarity with them has dulled our senses to the direct, raw pleading and complaining which is as necessary for a healthy faith as adoration.

In the wake of the tragedy at Dunblane Primary School in March 1996, a colleague said with evident dismay, "It's now I realize that we've forgotten how to lament." Perhaps the antidote to this feeling of inadequacy is to familiarize ourselves with the scriptural songs which Jesus knew by rote, and which for all time can offer the depth of human sorrow to the heart of God.

Thirdly, these—as all our songs—could never have been written were it not for our interaction with the people of God and with the Word of God. No material here was ever written "for publication." This book is the consequence of songs resonating in situations other than that for which they were first intended, rather than the goal behind our writing.
We believe that essentially a hymn should convey what God has to say to the people and/or what the people need to say to God. We are therefore keen to record our gratitude to those who have discussed the scriptures with us and shared those sorrows which informed our words.

The recording of THE LAST JOURNEY collection by The Cathedral Singers of Chicago afforded the opportunity to allow words and music for times of grieving to be presented in a choral medium. But there still remained the challenge to provide texts and tunes for all God's people. In response to that challenge, this book is offered.

The vast majority of the songs here have been arranged for congregational use. It is anticipated that they will be sung either *a cappella* or accompanied on keyboard or, occasionally, guitar. While several of the tunes may be new, most of the songs are in meters which allow for alternative melodies to be adopted.

However, that should not inhibit the occasional introduction of a new tune even at a requiem mass or funeral service. The authors of these texts well remember one such occasion when, because of the desire of a grieving congregation to articulate its sorrow, the hymn which was barely audible in verse 1, was sung with intensity by verse 5.

Nevertheless, there are occasions on which the depth of anguish which a people share makes their common voice weak. Then, an unobtrusive and sensitive individual may sing the words solo, while others follow the text. Or, if there is a choir in the church, the octavo arrangements of many of these texts may be worth putting into the vocabulary of the singers. A choir which functions well in a funeral situation is not one which has just "got up" an appropriate anthem. It is one where the conductor has the foresight to prepare the singers for all eventualities.

It is our hope that these songs may enable God's people to speak honestly to their Maker when grief is raw, just as other songs enable their praise to be represented when joy is deep.

John L. Bell
Graham Maule
Lent 1997

SONGS
FOR
THE TIME OF GRIEVING

Who is there to understand?

faltering, as the text demands ♩ = 60

CARRINGTON (JLB)

1. All the fears I need to name but am too scared to say;
2. All the wast - ed years in which I strug - gled to be free;
3. What the cause of pain is and, much more, the rea - son why;
4. "All the wrong you now ad - mit, I prom - ise to for - give;

all the shame for what I've done which noth - ing can al - lay;
all the bro - ken prom - is - es that took their toll on me;
what my fi - nal hour will bring, how sud - den - ly I'll die;
all that you re - gret, you are not sen - tenced to re - live;

all the peo - ple I've let down and lost a - long the way;
all the love I should have shown and all I failed to be;
what the fu - ture holds for those I'll miss, for whom I cry;
all the love you've nev - er known is mine a - lone to give;

For many people, grief is such a sudden and isolating experience that they feel no one can appreciate what they are going through. This song, based on the conversation of one such person moves from a statement of the human confusion to an intimation of God's response.

It should be sung solo, though a different voice would be appropriate for the final verse.

This song is featured in the CD/Cassette and Octavo collection entitled THE LAST JOURNEY. The individual octavo arrangement for keyboard, voice and cello may be found in the GIA catalog No.: G-4528.

How long, O Lord?

slow and bluesy ♩ = 54

NEW THIRTEENTH (JLB)
Text: Psalm 13 (para. JLB)

1. How long, O Lord, will you quite for - get
2. How long, O Lord, must this grief pos - sess my
3. Look now, look now and an - swer me, my

me? How long, O Lord, will you
heart? How long, O Lord, must I
God; give light, give light lest I

turn your face from me? How long, O
lan - guish night and day? How long, O
sleep the sleep of death. Lest my en -

However down and unhappy people feel, someone in the Bible will have been there before them. It is an immense source of consolation that all through the centuries Jews and Christians have sung their despair to God, using the words of the psalms.

When such poems are used, we stand in solidarity with a great host of believers, including Jesus, who found consolation in knowing that God could take all their questions and despair. This is another solo lament, though the congregation may be encouraged to join the final verse.

This song is featured in the CD/Cassette and Octavo Collections entitled THE LAST JOURNEY. The individual octavo arrangement for voice, keyboard and cello may be found in the GIA catalog No.: G-4531.

We cannot measure how you heal

gently ♩ = 90

YE BANKS AND BRAES Scots trad. (arr. JLB)

1. We can - not meas - ure how you heal or an - swer eve - ry suf - ferer's prayer, yet we be - lieve your grace re - sponds where faith and
2. The pain that will not go a - way, the guilt that clings from things long past, the fear be - of what the fu - ture holds, are pres - ent
3. So some have come who need your help and some have come to make a - mends, as hands which shaped and saved the world are pres - ent

Though originally written for use at service of healing, this song has been used to good effect in situations of loss and at requiem masses or funeral services. The tune, one of the most universally known Scottish traditional melodies, makes for effortless singing.

I cry to God

Tune: NEW 77TH (JLB)
Text: Psalm 77 (para. JLB)

lamentoso ♩ = 48

1. I cry to God and he hears me; in my
2. I think of God and I moan; I
3. I thought of days gone by, and re-
4. Will God re-ject us for-ev-er? Will
5. Has God for-got-ten to be gra-cious? Has
(6.) me now re-mem-ber God's work and re-

times of troub-le I seek him. By
med-i-tate and feel use-less. God
mem-bered times now van-ished. I
God re-fuse us his mer-cy? Has
an-ger doused his com-pas-sion? Has God's
call his won-der-ful great-ness. Let me

night   my   hands   plead   in prayer,   but   I
keeps   the   sleep   from   my eyes,   and   my
spent   the   night   in deep dis - tress   while my
end - less   love reached an end?   Are   God's
might - y   arm   lost   its grasp?   Does   it
med - i -   tate on   his power   and   re -

find   noth - ing   for   my   com - fort.
speech   is   lost   in   con - fu - sion.
spir - it mur - mured   with - in   me.
prom - is - es   now   in - val - id?
hang   pow - er - less   be - side   him?   6. Let
mem - ber all   God   has done.

This psalm is representative of the mood swings which people experience in times of grief. We believe...and yet we doubt; and we sense sometimes the absence of the God we want to affirm. Again, the consolation of Scripture is that such a reaction is nothing if not normal.

This song is featured in the CD/Cassette and Octavo collections entitled THE LAST JOURNEY. The individual Octavo arrangement for choir, organ, oboe and flute may be found in the GIA catalog No.: G-4530.

Word of the Father

gently ♩ = 90

Tune: WORD OF THE FATHER (JLB)

1. Word of the Father,

   Come, Lord, come;
   and take our fear away,
   and take our fear away;
   replace it with your love.

2. Firstborn of Mary,

3. Healer and helper,

4. Servant and sufferer,

5. Jesus, redeemer,

6. Christ resurrected,

7. Maranatha!

This simple call and response song may be sung *a cappella* in harmony or with a cantor and congregation accompanied by keyboard. It may be useful as a prelude to worship, an entrance song or a communion hymn.

SONGS
OF
CONSOLATION

A woman's care

Tune: *DIED FOR LOVE* English trad. (arr. JLB)
Text: *Isaiah Ch. 49 (para JLB)*

gently ♩. = 48

1. When troub - le strikes and fear takes root, and
2. Our wan - dering minds be - lieve the worst and
3. God says, "See how a wom - an cares. Can
4. "My dear - est daugh - ter, fond - est son, my
5. Then praise the Lord through faith and fear, in

dreams are dry and sense un - sound; when
ask, as faith and fer - vor fade, "Has
she for - get the child she bore? Even
wea - ry folk in eve - ry land, your
ho - ly and in hope - less place; for

Words and Arrangement: © 1987, 1996, WGRG, The Iona Community. GIA Publications, Inc., exclusive North American Agent.

hope be - comes a bar - ren waste, then
God now turned his back on us for -
if she did, I shan't for - get: though
souls are cra - dled in my heart, though your
height and depth and heaven and hell can't

doubts like moun - tains soar a - round.
sak - ing those he loved and made?"
feel - ing lost, I love you more."
names are writ - ten on my hand."
keep us far from God's em - brace.

From childhood, it is often our mother to whom we run in times of distress. There is something in the understanding of the mother which we feel we can trust. How appropriate, therefore, that God, in several passages of Isaiah's prophecy, should speak of the divine self in terms of a woman, a midwife and a mother.

If this is being sung by a congregation, the women should sing verses 3 & 4 on their own.

An alternative tune in Long Meter is ROCKINGHAM.

God was there

moderato 𝅗𝅥 = 54

ROBERTSON (JLB)

1. When the wind on cha - os blew,
2. Where the ear - liest mor - tals talked,
3. While the trades - man was de - cried,
4. God was there but not in vain.
5. In each dark - ness, cloud and fire,
6. Not for what we are or do,

when the world from noth - ing grew, when the pri - mal
where the vir - gin land was walked, where e - mer - gent
while the sav - ior was de - nied, while his son was
Shield - ing joy and shar - ing pain, rais - ing life to
in the quiet as words re - tire, in our loss and
not for what we've jour - neyed through, but for all you

dream came true, God was there.
faith was rocked, God was there.
cru - ci - fied, God was there.
live a - gain, God was there.
best de - sire, God is there.
call us to, God, be there.

If one were to write a history of God, it would be one in which God's love does not provide a safe cocoon, but rather demands risk and vulnerability. The Bible repeatedly offers us insights into the heart of God which hurts, yearns and weeps until, in Jesus, God takes flesh and lives in solidarity with us that we might know that nothing can separate us from his love.

Be still and know that I am God

quietly but steadily ♩ = 54

Tune: BE STILL (JLB)
Text: Psalm 46, verse 10

This simple chant can be sung solo or in canon with another voice, or the congregation may be invited to join in the singing.

This song is featured in the CD/Cassette and Octavo Collections entitled GOD NEVER SLEEPS. The individual octavo arrangement for two soloists and choir may be found in the GIA catalog No.: G-4382.

Let your restless hearts be still

very gently ♩ = 60

Tune: THE LARK IN THE CLEAR AIR Irish trad. (arr. JLB)
Text: John 14 (para. JLB)

1. Let your rest - less hearts be still, let your
troub - led minds be rest - ed; trust in God to lift your
care and, in car - ing, trust in me. In God's

2. Where I am and where I'll be, is where
you shall live for - ev - er; and the way to where I
go I have walked a - mong you here. I'm the

This is a solo song which may be sung during a funeral service or on some other occasion when the assurance of Christ's peace is of utmost importance.

This song is featured in the CD/Cassette and Octavo collections entitled THE LAST JOURNEY. The individual octavo arrangement for soloist and choir may be found in the GIA catalog No.: G-4532.

Sing, my soul

Tune: MYSIE (JLB)

gently ♩ = 72

1. Sing, my soul, when hope is sleep - ing, sing when faith gives way to fears; sing to melt the ice of sad - ness, mak - ing way for joy through tears.

2. Sing, my soul, when sick - ness lin - gers, sing to dull the sharp - est pain; sing to set the spir - it leap - ing: heal - ing needs a glad re - frain.

3. Sing, my soul, of him who shaped me, let me wan - der far a - way, ran with o - pen arms to greet me, brought me home a - gain to stay.

4. Sing, my soul, when light seems dark - est, sing when night re - fus - es rest, sing though death should mock the fu - ture: what's to come by God is blessed.

This essentially solo song is a paraphrase of a letter from an elderly saintly woman whose testimony is that, even in her lowest days, when she speaks to God, he listens. Then she sings to rejoice both her heart and his. It is well suit-ed to the Saturday of Holy Week or to other occasions when loss or weakness is evident.

SONGS
FOR
GOD'S HELP

Since we are summoned

very gently ♩ = 52

Tune: SILENT PLACE (JLB)

1. Since we are sum-moned to a
2. Since we are sav-aged by the
3. Since we are forced to face this
4. Christ be be-neath us, Christ be

si-lent place, strug-gling to find some words to
pain of loss, stopped at a bar-rier we have
last fare-well, sad-dened to depths we nev-er
all a-bove, Christ take the hand of *her* we've

fill the space; Christ be be-side us as we grieve,
yet to cross; Christ be be-side us as we mourn,
could fore-tell; Christ be be-side us as we weep,
lost and love; take her to par-a-dise and then

dar - ing to doubt or to be - lieve.
bro - ken, dis - con - so - late and torn.
loos - 'ning our hold on whom you'll keep.
Christ be be - side us once a - gain.

For some people, the Silent Place may be the church or the funeral home, or the room in their home where they have to come to terms with unwanted loss. Drawing on the words of people who have been in that place, this song articulates their deep longings.

This song is featured in the CD/Cassette and Octavo collections entitled THE LAST JOURNEY. The individual octavo arrangement for choir, keyboard and cello may be found in the GIA catalog No.: G-4536.

O Christ, you wept

gently ♩ = 60

Tune: PALMER (JLB)

1. O Christ, you wept when grief was raw, and felt for those who mourned their friend; come close to where we would not be and
2. The well-loved voice is silent now and we have much we meant to say; come collect our lost and wandering words and
3. We try to hold what is not here and fear for what we do not know; oh take our hands in yours, Good Lord, and
4. In all our loneliness and doubt through what we cannot realize, oh address us from your empty tomb and

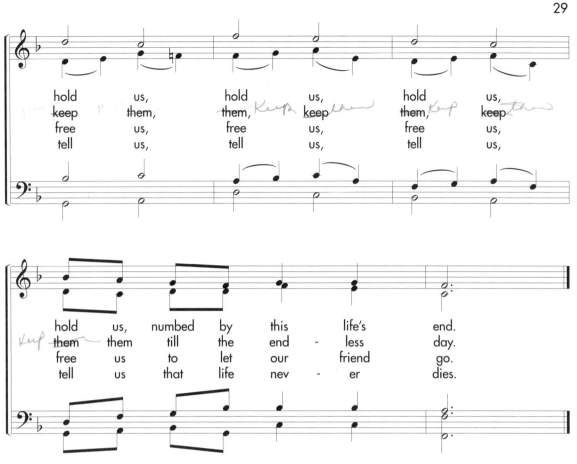

The shortest verse in the Bible, 'Jesus wept' appears in the 11th chapter of John's gospel where the sorrow of the sisters and friends of Lazarus brings Jesus himself to tears. If anyone ever wondered whether Christ really had a human heart, this story is ample proof.

This song is featured in the CD/Cassette and Octavo Collections entitled THE LAST JOURNEY. The individual octavo arrangement for choir, keyboard and flute may be found in the GIA catalog No.: G-4529.

God give us life

quietly but firmly ♩ = 65

Tune: CAMPBELL (JLB)

1. God give us life when all a-round spells death and none are clear that hope is died; and
2. God give us love in heart and hand to hold and the some have find, where the an - ger, meet is the
3. God give us skill in - sight and will to find, death un - sheath its new threads to mend the web of
4. God give us faith, should all else fail and death give us strength to sting. O help us hear, through pain and
5. Then, in the end, make death a friend, and hurt - ing are its sure, un - some have stand and walk to where no eye can

near   or   fate   can   be   de - fied.
need   and   wait   till   wait - ing's done.
life,   new   means   to   heal   and   cure.
fear,   the   songs   that   an - gels sing.
stare,   but   Christ   can   clasp   our   hand.

When one of our friends was dying from cancer, it became evident that there were more people to pray for than the patient. Those who visited, those who cared professionally, those who were involved in medical research—all these and more are involved in the drama of life beginning and ending and beginning again.

Each verse of this song, therefore, allows for different people to be prayed for.

A touching place

tenderly ♩. = 48

Tune: DREAM ANGUS Scots trad. (arr. JLB)

1. Christ's is the world in which we move,
2. Feel for the peo - ple we most a - void,
3. Feel for the par - ents who've lost their child,
4. Feel for the lives by life con - fused,

Christ's are the folk we're sum - moned to love,
strange or be - reaved or nev - er em - ployed;
feel for the wom - en whom men have de - filed,
rid - dled with doubt, in lov - ing a - bused;

Christ's is the voice which calls us to care, and
feel for the wom - en and feel for the men who
feel for the ba - by for whom there's no breast, and
feel for the lone - ly heart, con - scious of sin, which

This, which is one of our earliest songs, was written to enable the healing service in Iona Abbey. The words draw on the great Celtic theme of the Incarnate Christ who did and always will touch his people, and the tune is that of a Gaelic lullaby...a woman's working song.

This song is featured in the CD/Cassette and Octavo Collections entitled GOD NEVER SLEEPS. The individual octavo arrangement for soloist and choir may be found in the GIA catalog No.: G-4377.

Calm in the storm

steadily ♩= 48

Tune: CALM IN THE STORM (JLB)

1. Calm in the storm, foot-path and friend in the dark,
2. Where faith is low, where hope has noth-ing to show,
3. Lives bruised and torn, ba-bies a-bout to be born,
4. Calm in the storm, foot-path and friend in the dark,

song in the night, trust-ing your touch in-to your
where love is spent; there show your face, there let your
folk near-ing death— send each an an-gel or a
song in the night, glo-ry to you, Sav-ior and

care we com-mit those hid from sight.
heav-en-ly grace fond-ly be sent.
word or a sign warm with your breath.
Lord, strength and shield, lift-er and light.

The promise of Christian faith is not that those who believe will have an easy life, but that in every difficulty they face, God will not abandon them. Hence, Jesus does not avoid the storm, but accompanies his disciples through it.

SONGS
OF
LEAVE TAKING

The last journey

moderato ♩ = 80

IONA BOAT SONG Scots trad. (arr. JLB)

1. From the fal-ter of breath, through the si-lence of death, to the won-der that's break-ing be-yond; God has wo-ven a
2. From frus-tra-tion and pain, through hope hard to sus-tain, to the whole-ness here prom-ised, there known; Christ has gone where we
3. From the dim-ming of light, through the dark-ness of night, to the glo-ry of good-ness a-bove; God the Spir-it is
4. From to-day till we die, through all ques-tion-ing why, to the place from which time and tide flow; an-gels tread on our

Legend has it that this tune was used as ancient Scottish kings were, after death, rowed to their resting place on the island of Iona. It would be a pity if such a fine tune were reserved solely for the use of royalty.

This song is featured in the CD/Cassette and Octavo Collections entitled THE LAST JOURNEY. The individual octavo arrangement for choir, flute and cello may be found in the GIA catalog No.: G-4535.

Go, silent friend

warmly ♩ = 45

Tune: Psalm12 LONDONDERRY AIR (arr. JLB)

1. Go, si-lent friend, your life has found its end-ing; to dust re-
2. Go, si-lent friend, for-give us if we grieved you; safe now in

turns your wea-ry mor-tal frame. God, who be-fore birth
heav-en, kind-ly say our name. Your life has touched us,

called you in-to be-ing, now calls you hence, his ac-cent still the
that is why we mourn you; our lives with-out you can-not be the

Lyrics:

Verse 1: same. Go, si-lent friend, your life in Christ is bur-ied; for you he lived and died and rose a-gain. Close by his side your prom-ised place is wait-ing, where, ful-ly known, you shall with God re-main.

Verse 2: same. Go, si-lent friend, we do not grudge you glo-ry; sing, sing with joy deep prais-es to your Lord. You, who be-lieved that Christ would come back for you, now cel-e-brate that Je-sus keeps his word.

Go, silent friend

firmly ♩ = 80

Tune: Psalm 12 DONNE SECOURS (arr. JLB)

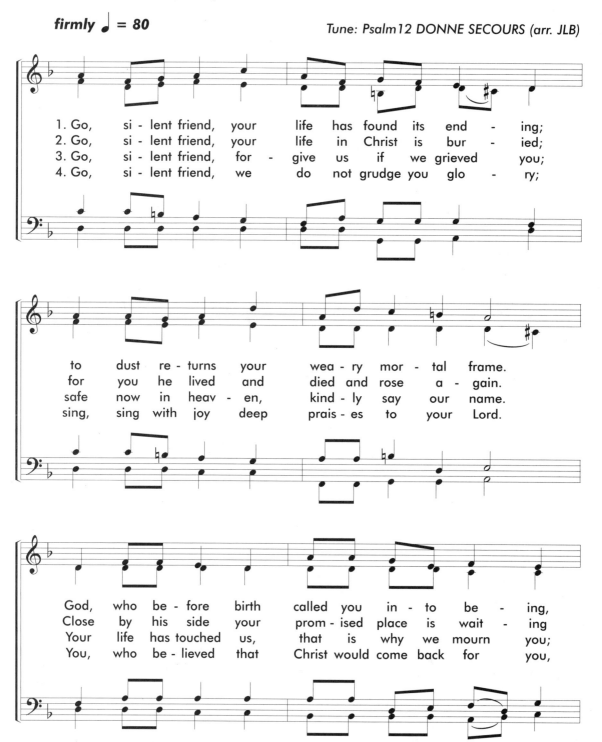

1. Go, si - lent friend, your life has found its end - ing;
2. Go, si - lent friend, your life in Christ is bur - ied;
3. Go, si - lent friend, for - give us if we grieved you;
4. Go, si - lent friend, we do not grudge you glo - ry;

to dust re - turns your wea - ry mor - tal frame.
for you he lived and died and rose a - gain.
safe now in heav - en, kind - ly say our name.
sing, sing with joy deep prais - es to your Lord.

God, who be - fore birth called you in - to be - ing,
Close by his side your prom - ised place is wait - ing
Your life has touched us, that is why we mourn you;
You, who be - lieved that Christ would come back for you,

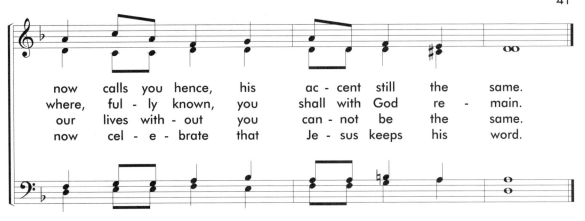

now   calls   you hence,   his   ac - cent still   the   same.
where, ful - ly known,   you   shall with God   re -   main.
our   lives with - out   you   can - not be   the   same.
now   cel - e - brate   that   Je - sus keeps his   word.

The text was originally written for the funeral of an unassuming saint of God, a former cleaning woman who had risked her life during the Nazi occupation of Amsterdam by looking after a Jewish fugitive as if she were a member of the family. This is a song of farewell, most appropriate towards the end of a funeral service or as the casket leaves the church. The tune PSALM 12 (DONNE SECOURS) is a beautiful early reformation melody, possibly showing signs of earlier secular dance use. The alternative is arguably the best known traditional Irish melody.

This song is featured in the CD/Cassette and Octavo collections entitled THE LAST JOURNEY. The individual octavo arrangement for soloist, quartet and choir may be found in the GIA catalog No.: G-4537.

He is not here

positively ♩ = 55

Tune: COISRIGEADH Scots trad. (arr. JLB)

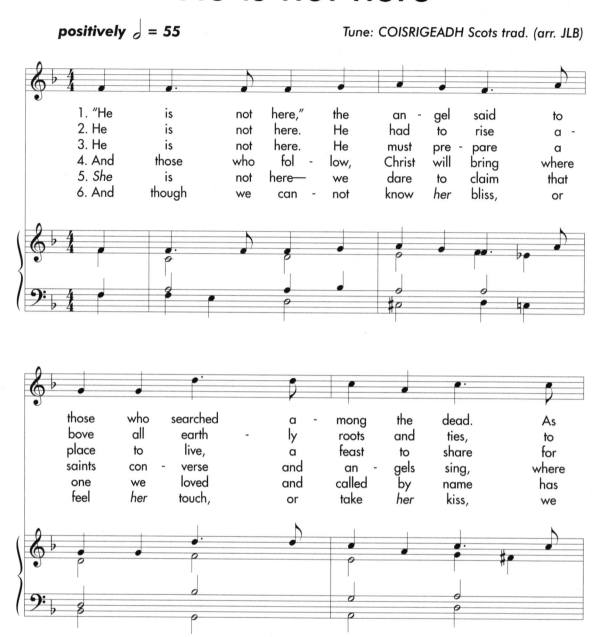

1. "He is not here," the an-gel said to
2. He is not here. He had to rise a-
3. He is not here. He must pre-pare a
4. And those who fol-low, Christ will bring where
5. *She* is not here— we dare to claim that
6. And though we can-not know *her* bliss, or

those who searched a - mong the dead. As
bove all earth - ly roots and ties, to
place to live, a feast to share for
saints con - verse and an - gels sing, where
one we loved and called by name has
feel *her* touch, or take *her* kiss, we

This song, also for the conclusion of a funeral rite, links the death and resurrection of Christ with that of his disciples. Please note that, depending on the circumstances, 'she' and 'her' in verses 5 & 6 can be changed to he/his/him or they/their/them. An alternative tune in Long Meter is WINCHESTER NEW.

For all the saints

moderato ♩ = 70

Tune: O WALY WALY English trad. (arr. JLB)

1. For all the saints who showed your
2. For all the saints who loved your
3. For all the saints who named your
4. Bless all whose will or name or

love in how they live and where they
name, whose faith in - creased the Sav - ior's
will, and saw your king - dom com - ing
love re - flects the grace of heaven a -

moved, for mind - ful wom - en, car - ing
fame, who sang your songs and shared your
still through self - less pro - test, prayer and
bove. Though un - ac - claimed by earth - ly

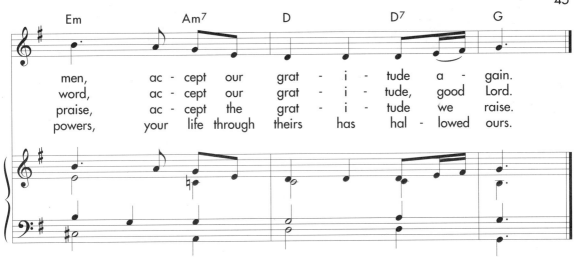

This is a simple song of gratitude which may be appropriate, depending on the circumstances, at funeral or memorial services, or around All Saints Day.

This song is featured on the CD/Cassette and Octavo Collections entitled THE LAST JOURNEY. The individual octavo arrangement for choir, oboe and keyboard may be found in the GIA catalog No.: G-4540.

Stay with us now

steadily ♩ = 60

Tune: DARKNESS (JLB)

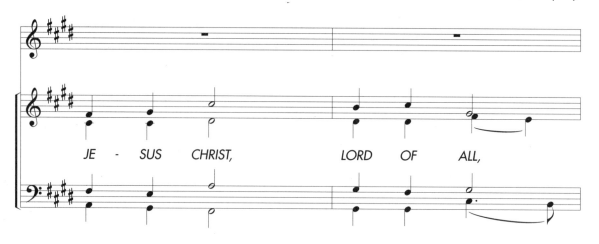

JE - SUS CHRIST,   LORD   OF   ALL,

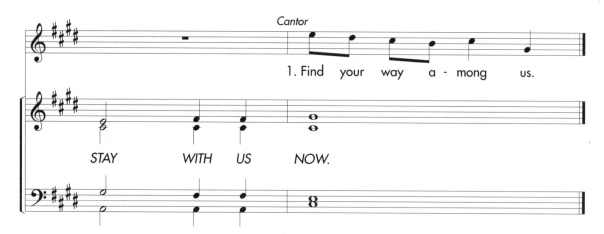

Cantor

1. Find your way a - mong us.

STAY   WITH   US   NOW.

2. Listen to the anxious.

3. Sit beside the lonely.

4. Comfort the despairing.

5. Out of love and mercy,

6. Do not ever leave us.

7. Even when we doubt you,

8. Maker of tomorrow,

This simple call and response song is flexible in its use, and allows for improvised petitions, depending on the circumstances.

SONGS
FOR
SPECIAL CIRCUMSTANCES

A cradling song

very tenderly ♩ = 70

Tune: JENNIFER (JLB)

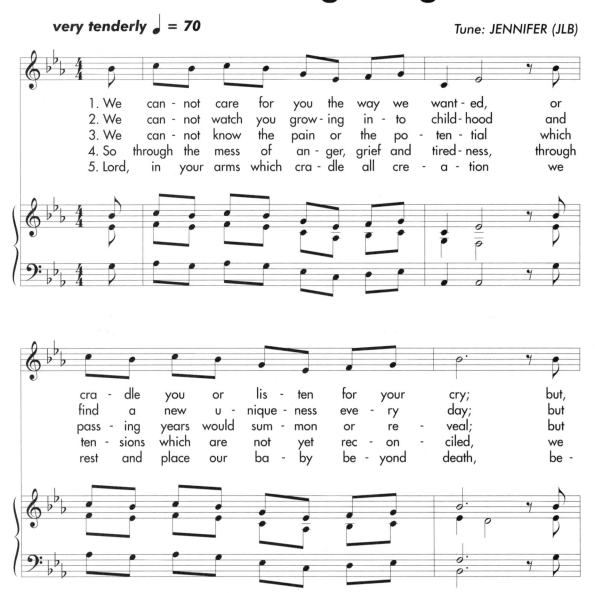

1. We can-not care for you the way we want-ed, or
2. We can-not watch you grow-ing in-to child-hood and
3. We can-not know the pain or the po-ten-tial which
4. So through the mess of an-ger, grief and tired-ness, through
5. Lord, in your arms which cra-dle all cre-a-tion we

cra-dle you or lis-ten for your cry; but,
find a new u-nique-ness eve-ry day; but
pass-ing years would sum-mon or re-veal; but
ten-sions which are not yet rec-on-ciled, we
rest and place our ba-by be-yond death, be-

sep - a - rat - ed   as   we   are   by   si - lence,
spe - cial   as   you   would   have   been   a - mong   us,
for   that   true   ful - fil - ment   Je - sus   prom - ised
give   to   God   the   wor - ship   of   our   sor - row
liev - ing   that *she* now,   a - live   in   heav - en,

1.-4.

love   will   not   die.
you   still   will   stay.
we   hope   and   feel.
and   our   dear   child.

5.

breathes   with   your   breath.

The death of a child in the womb during pregnancy, or the birth of a stillborn child, or the gradual fading from life of a tiny baby brings feelings of anger, desolation and deep disappointment which have no parallel in the grief over a friend whose life has run its full course. It is unlikely that any community of people would wish to sing this song. It is best sung by a soloist, though the words—if printed—may be of comfort to those most affected.

50

There is a place

very gently ♩ = 60

Tune: DUNBLANE PRIMARY (JLB)

1. There is a place prepared for little children, those we once lived for, those we deeply mourn, those who from play, from learning and from

2. There is a place where hands which held ours tightly now are released beyond all hurt and fear, healed by that love which also feels our

3. There is a place where all the lost potential yields its full promise, finds its true intent; silenced no more, young voices echo

4. There is a place where God will hear our questions, suffer our anger, share our speechless grief, gently repair the innocence of

5. Jesus, who bids us be like little children, shields those our arms are yearning to embrace. God will ensure that all are reu-

This song was written in memory of the sixteen primary school children and their teacher who were killed by a gunman at 9:30 a.m. on Wednesday, 13th March, 1996, in Dunblane, Scotland. It was never intended as a congregational hymn, though it may be used as such. Its original choral setting allows for reflection on the text which is not possible if everyone is involved in singing.

This song is featured in the CD/Cassette and Octavo collections entitled THE LAST JOURNEY. The individual octavo arrangement for choir and organ is available in the GIA catalog No.: G-4542.

What shall we pray?

Tune: KINGSTON (JLB)
Text: (Carnwadric Parish Church Worship Group and JLB)

gently ♩ = 70

1. What shall we pray for those who died,
2. What shall we pray for those who mourn
3. What shall we pray for those who live
4. What shall we pray for those who know
5. What shall we pray for those who fear
6. God give us peace and, more than this,

those on whose death our lives re- lied?
friend- ships and love, their fruit un- born?
tied to the past they can't for- give,
noth- ing of war, and can- not show
war, in some guise, may re- ap- pear
show us the path where jus- tice is;

Si- lenced by war but not de- nied,
Though years have passed, hearts still are torn;
haunt- ed by ter- rors they re- live?
grief or re- gret for friend or foe?
look- ing at- trac- tive and sin- cere?
and let us nev- er be re- miss

God give them peace.
God give them peace.
God give them peace.
God give them peace.
God give them peace.
work - ing for peace that lasts.

In Scotland, Remembrance Sunday, when the nation honors those who have died in war, can be a fraught occasion. It brings back unspeakably painful memories to some, offends others, and puzzles younger people who have only seen pictures of war. In this song, representatives of a local congregation identified the different people who would be reacting to services of remembrance, holding them together before God with the same prayer.

As if you were not there

solemnly ♩ = 60

Tune: ILICH (JLB)

1. As if you were not there, the skies ig - nite and
2. As if you were not there, fam - ine and flood to -
3. As if you were not there, we tel - e - vise the
4. As if you were not there, your Son, when faith de -
5. Be - cause he rose a - gain and showed God's love is

thun - der, riv - ers tear their banks a -
geth - er ush - er death, dis - ease and
dy - ing, watch the help - less vic - tims
fied him, faced a crowd which cru - ci -
vast - er than the ul - ti - mate dis -

sun - der, thieves and na - ture storm and plun - der: all be -
ter - ror; strick - en moth - ers won - der wheth - er God heeds
cry - ing, salve our con - scienc - es by sigh - ing "Life's un -
fied him, leav - ing friends who had de - nied him in de -
as - ter, we en - treat you now to mas - ter strife and

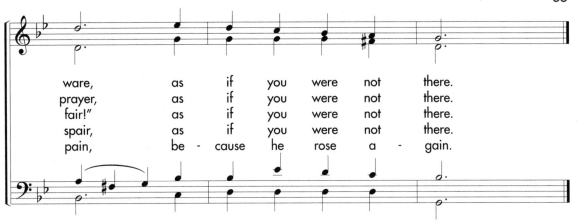

ware,	as	if	you	were	not	there.
prayer,	as	if	you	were	not	there.
fair!"	as	if	you	were	not	there.
spair,	as	if	you	were	not	there.
pain,	be - cause	he	rose	a -	gain.	

Though most of this collection deals with grieving for people known to us, the Church, if it is the Body of Christ, has to share the pain of those we do not necessarily see, but who are bound to us in Christ. So this song and the following one offer lament and prayer for people and places in the world beyond our shores. What is euphemistically called "natural disaster" lies behind the text of this song.

Listen, Lord

firmly ♩ = 60

Tune: LISTEN, LORD (JLB)

LIS-TEN, LORD. LIS-TEN, LORD, NOT TO OUR WORDS BUT TO OUR PRAYER.

Fine

YOU A-LONE, YOU A-LONE, UN-DER-STAND AND CARE.

1. Where the voice that once was wel - come
2. Where the wis - dom meant to heal is
3. Where the with - ered hands and hopes stretch
4. Turn the world and spurn the spite of

sounds no more, send your love to
spent to harm, rouse the smoth - ered
out in vain, burst the store - house
hu - man greed; train our a - dult

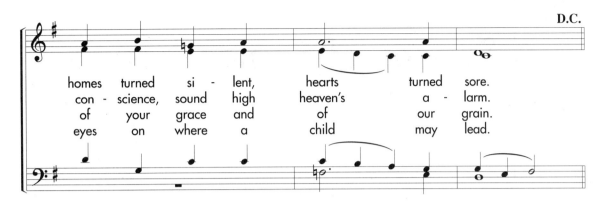

homes	turned	si -	lent,	hearts	turned	sore.
con -	science,	sound	high	heaven's	a -	larm.
of	your	grace	and	of	our	grain.
eyes	on	where	a	child	may	lead.

If the previous song dealt with the consequences of natural disasters, then this text deals with the grim reality that death in developing countries through war, malnutrition and disease can also be related to the economic or cultural imperialism, the need for arms sales and the overconsumption of raw materials and food which is a feature of life in the "civilized" West. It is best that this song be sung with a choir, quartet or soloist taking the verses.

A Service of Remembering

FOREWORD

The following may be used in its complete form as an Order of Worship for remembering those who have died, or extracts from it may be employed in association with local material and intentions. Some sections, for example *There Is a Place,* may be relevant in communities coping with the death of infants. In other places it might better be omitted.

The musical material comes almost exclusively from this book *(WGIR),* and the associated collections of anthems, *The Last Journey (L J).* The availability of a choir and the extent of their repertoire and ability will dictate what proportion should be given over to performers, what shared with the congregation, and whether better known materials may occasionally be incorporated.

Any teaching of new material should either be done by a cantor before the commencement of worship, or by having the first verses of unfamiliar songs sung solo.

It is envisaged that the service proceed without announcement, and that the published text be used only by those leading the worship. Members of the Assembly can have the relevant extracts or song texts published in an appropriate brochure.

In situations where there is a good audio system but no choir, tracks from *The Last Journey* CD recording may be played.

Five people are envisaged in leadership roles:
   Leader who may be the priest or pastoral figure involved in funerals and bereavement
      counseling;
   2 Readers who should speak from the front of the Assembly;
   2 Voices who should speak from the rear or sides of the assembly.

It is suggested that because many people find signs as or more helpful than words, opportunity may be given towards the end of the service for the lighting of candles, writing of names, placing of petals or flowers as is appropriate.

Finally, because there is an amazing solidarity in grief, it is respectfully suggested that communities using this kind of service might enable the Assembly to share refreshments and conversation afterwards.

John L. Bell
The Iona Community
September 1997

ORDER OF WORSHIP

INTRODUCTION

Assembly Song	"O Christ, You Wept"
Prayer	
Antiphonal Reading	Psalm 90

God Is Big Enough

Solo	"Who Is There to Understand?"
Solo/Assembly	"How Long, O Lord?"

The Love Which Heals

Assembly	"We Cannot Measure"

Last Words

Choir	"Let Your Restless Hearts Be Still"
Assembly	"Word of the Father"

You Have Been Here Before

Choir	"Steal Away"
Assembly	"Be Still"

The Last Journey

Choir & Assembly	"The Last Journey"

Called Home

Choir & Assembly	"Lord our God, Receive Your Servant"
Assembly	"Go, Silent Friend"

A Glimpse of Heaven

Choir	"In Zion"
Assembly	"He Is Not Here"

There Is a Place

Choir/Assembly	"There Is a Place"
Solo	"A Cradling Song"

For All the Saints

Scripture	
Time of Remembering	
Prayer	
Assembly	"For All the Saints"

Blessing

Choir	"Nobody Knows"

INTRODUCTION

Leader: This is not a place meant only for sadness.
It is the House of God built for praise;
and it is the best place to offer the worship of our sorrow,
and to feel for the solidarity of the saints
who always made for heaven
through the suffering of life on earth.

God does not guarantee a painless life.

The bones of dinosaurs who walked the earth millions of years
before men and women, show evidence of cancer.
There have always been fault lines in creation.

The issue is not how to escape hurt, but how to handle it.

The Gospel directs us to God who in Christ feels pain,
and faces death and goes through these realities.

And he does this to show that death is not the end,
and he does it promising to be present to those in every age
who wait and weep and watch and pray.

Voice 1: What did they think, Lord,
those who watched you cry
in front of women,
in front of men,
for your dead friend,
or your favorite city?

Did they admire your tenderness
having seen your toughness?
Were they disgusted by your tears
and loss of self control?
Or were they drawn into your sorrow
for the plight of the world
and the pain of its people?

For, Christ,
you wept
when grief was raw.

ASSEMBLY SONG: "O Christ, You Wept" *(WGIR & L J)*

PRAYER:

Leader: Let us pray.

O God our maker,
against the backcloth of your everlastingness,
we, creatures of a day,
live and move and have our being.

Here we acknowledge
that while life may be random,
it is not futile.

You have purposed us
for a future
which we, limited by flesh and blood,
cannot imagine.

Yet in Jesus,
who brought eternity into touch with time,
we see glimpses of the greater life
for which we strive
and into which others have entered.

Surround us here
not with shallow sentiment which vanishes,
but with a deep sense
of your compassion for us
and of your embrace
on all those we no longer can touch.

Assure us that they are in good company
and that we, in this holy place,
are in good hands.

We pray in Jesus' name.
AMEN.

READING: Psalm 90 *(Grail version)*

Voice 1:   Lord, you have been our refuge
              from one generation to the next.
All: BEFORE THE MOUNTAINS WERE BORN
              OR THE EARTH OR THE WORLD BROUGHT FORTH,
              YOU ARE GOD, WITHOUT BEGINNING OR END.

Voice 2:   You turn us back to dust
              and say, "Go back, children of the earth."
All: TO YOUR EYES A THOUSAND YEARS
              ARE LIKE YESTERDAY, COME AND GONE,
              NO MORE THAN A WATCH IN THE NIGHT.
Voice 1:   You sweep us away like a dream,
              like grass which springs up in the morning.
All: IN THE MORNING IT SPRINGS UP AND FLOWERS;
              BY EVENING IT WITHERS AND FADES.

Voice 2:   Make us know the shortness of our life
              that we may gain wisdom of heart.
All: IN THE MORNING FILL US WITH YOUR LOVE,
              SO THAT WE CAN REJOICE ALL OUR DAYS.

Voice 1:   Give us joy to balance our affliction
              for the years when we knew misfortune.
All: SHOW FORTH YOUR WORK TO YOUR SERVANTS;
              LET YOUR GLORY SHINE ON THEIR CHILDREN.

God Is Big Enough

Reader A: Bessie Brown was old when she told the story
              of how, in the 50's, she had gone to a funeral.

              A woman had been killed in a car crash,
              leaving three young children and a distraught husband.

              The mourners had gathered in the house,
              gathered round the coffin,
              waiting for the pastor to come and say prayers.

              Eventually, the door swung open.
              In swooped the pastor proclaiming,
              "She is not here! She is risen."

"I wanted to punch him in the face." said Bessie.

"We were not in any doubt of the general resurrection of the dead.
We needed to ask, Why *her* and why *now* and what's going to happen
to the children?"

(pause)

And God is big enough.
God is big enough to take our anger, our questions,
our doubt as well as our guilt.
And perhaps unless we say "Why?"
or "Where are you, God?" or
"Who is there to understand?"
we will never be able to sing Hallelujah.

SOLO: "Who Is There to Understand?" (WGIR & L J)
or
ASSEMBLY SONG: "How Long, O Lord" (WGIR & L J) verse 1 & 2 solo, verse 3 all

The Love Which Heals

Reader B: Gabby de Wille is a saint of God who lives in Belgium.
For most of her life she worked in a brassiere shop.
Hospitals used to send women to her who were told
        they had to have mastectomies.
Inevitably they would burst into tears.
Inevitably they would say that they feared
that if they had a mastectomy
their husband might not love them anymore.

Every time Gabby responded with the same words:
"Listen. If your husband really loves you
when you have two breasts,
he will love you twice as much,
when you only have one."
Every time, where love was deep,
the prophecy came true.

This is how God loves—twice as much
when we are unloved or unlovely or unloveable.
No. More than twice as much.
For we cannot measure how God heals.

ASSEMBLY SONG: "We Cannot Measure" *(WGIR)* verse 1 solo, verse 2 choir, verse 3 all (a cappella)

Last Word

Voice 2:
In an upstairs room,
surrounded by friends,
on the night that he was betrayed,
after his head had been anointed with oil,
while the table was set in presence of his enemies,
before his cup overflowed,
in the face of betrayal,
in expectation of denial,
as the jaws of hell began to wrench open,
when the past seemed irrelevant
because the future spelled the end;
with tension brimming around,
but with perfect calm within,
he spoke:

Voice 1:
"Let your restless hearts be still.
I'm going to prepare a place for you.
I'll come back to take you to where I will be."

SOLO/CHOIR: "Let Your Restless Hearts" *(WGIR & L J)*
or
CANTOR/ASSEMBLY: "Word of the Father" *(WGIR)*

You Have Been Here Before

Reader A:
Though hope deserts my heart,
though strangeness fills my soul,
though light evades my troubled mind,
you have been here before.

Though confidence runs dry,
though weary flesh is sore,
though conversation bears no fruit,
you have been here before.

There is no threatening place,
no trial I would forgo
which has not known your presence first;
you have been here before.

In Christ, who on the cross,
felt all our hurt and more,
and cried in deep abandonment,
you have been here before.
I will not fear the dark,
the fate beyond control;
fear must rein in frightening things;
you will be there before.

CHOIR: "Steal Away" (L J)
or
SOLO/ASSEMBLY: "Be Still and Know" (WGIR)

The Last Journey

Leader: At the turn of the century,
a commercial traveller was watching children play at funerals.
At the front were two boys with their hands tucked under their chins.
They were the well groomed horses pulling the cortege.
Behind them, two other boys carried a little girl,
who was lying stock still on a plank.
She was the corpse; they were the pall bearers.
Behind them a tall boy walked solemnly like an undertaker.
He was followed by a fat boy with a bible—the priest.
And at the rear came a crowd of children
sniffling into imaginary handkerchiefs—the mourners.
Thinking that he should play along with them,
the traveller approached the first boy who passed him,
one of those with his hands tucked under his chin.

"Who's dead?" asked the traveller.
"How should I know?" came the reply.
"I'm just a horse."
And as the boy slowly trotted past him,
he mused, "Maybe the important thing
is not knowing who's dead,
but being sure that there's a journey."

CHOIR AND/OR ASSEMBLY: "The Last Journey" (WGIR & L J)

Called Home

Reader B: It is the first day of November,
and the fall is giving way to winter.
Soon the trees will lose the vibrant colors of their leaves
and the snow will cover the ground.

The earth will shut down,
and people will race to and from their destinations
bundled up for warmth.
Chicago winters are harsh.
It is a time of dying.
But we know that spring will soon come
with all its new life and wonder.
It is quite clear that I will not be alive in the spring.
But I will soon experience new life in a different way.
Although I do not know what to expect in the afterlife,
I do know that just as God has called me
to serve him to the best of my abilities
throughout my life on earth,
he is now calling me home.

—Joseph Cardinal Bernardin
died November 14, 1996
Requiescet in pacem.

CHOIR & ASSEMBLY: "Lord Our God, Receive Your Servant" (L J)
or
ASSEMBLY: "Go, Silent Friend" /Londonderry Air (WGIR)

A Glimpse of Heaven

Reader A: When Jack Robertson was very small,
he used to ask his grandmother about heaven.
"Heaven?" she would reply.
"I'll tell you about heaven.
When you get to heaven there will be three surprises in store for you.
The first will be seeing all the people who *are* there.
The second will be realizing all the people who *aren't* there.
And the third—will be discovering that you're there yourself."

CHOIR: "In Zion" *(L J)*
or
ASSEMBLY: "He Is Not Here" *(WGIR)*

There Is a Place

Leader: On Wednesday February 13, 1996, at 9:30 am,
in the small cathedral town of Dunblane, Scotland,
a gunman entered the school gymnasium
and killed sixteen infants and their teacher
and wounded and mentally scarred many others.
And all the protests of innocence from the gun lobby,
and all the accusations of guilt from the bereaved,
and all the legislation for safety in schools,
and all the litigation for loss,
will not bring back the innocents
who were annihilated by evil.
Where are they now?
Simply at rest?
Always remembered?
Or is there a place?

CHOIR/ASSEMBLY: "There Is a Place" *(WGIR/L J)*
or
SOLO: "A Cradling Song" *(WGIR)*

SCRIPTURE READING

Reader B: Romans 8:31-35, 37-39

For All the Saints

Leader: We are who we are today
and we are where we are today,
because of those whose lives have touched ours
and who have let our lives touch theirs.

God, in the magnificence of things,
does not intend us to be neutral
when we lose those who have loved us.

So, our grief has to be tinged with gratitude
 for lives which have shaped us,
 for hands that have held us,
 for voices that have inspired us,
 for eyes which have beheld us,
 for ears that have listened to us.

Believing that those who have died in Christ
are risen with Christ,
we trust that we will meet again
in a place where there can never be farewells.

So, let us together make silent prayers
or visible signs of our affection
for those who now share in the closer harmony of heaven.

*(Here, silence may be kept or candles lit, or petals laid around a stand-
ing cross etc., as suits the space and occasion. Instrumental music may
be played, or if a repeated chant can be sung, "Listen Lord" from* Come
All You People *may be appropriate.)*

PRAYER

Leader: Let us pray.

Eternal God,
you see face to face
those whom we remember here.

Tell them that we love them,
  that we miss them,
  that they are not forgotten.

And, cheered by the prospect of a day
 when there will be no more death or parting
 and all shall be well and all shall be one,
if it be your will,
may they, whom we remember,
be among the first to welcome us to heaven.
And until that day,
when in the company of the blessed Virgin Mary
and all the saints,
we share in the everlasting feast of Christ's family,

keep us in faith,
fill us with hope,
deepen us through love,
to the glory of your holy name.
AMEN.

ASSEMBLY SONG: "For All the Saints" *(WGIR & L J)*

BLESSING

Leader:	On our heads and our houses,
All:	THE BLESSING OF GOD.
Leader:	In our coming and going,
All:	THE PEACE OF GOD.
Leader:	In our life and believing,
All:	THE LOVE OF GOD.
Leader:	At our end and new beginning,
All:	THE ARMS OF GOD TO WELCOME US AND BRING US HOME.
	AMEN.

CHOIR: "Nobody Knows" *(L J)*

Alphabetical index of first lines

Associated publications

Many of the songs in this book have been recorded by The Cathedral Singers of Chicago and appear in the CD/Cassette entitled THE LAST JOURNEY. As well as the original texts and tunes printed here, THE LAST JOURNEY recording with its associated octavo pack of the same name, includes settings of spirituals from the USA and Africa, as well as through-composed anthems based on scriptural and liturgical texts associated with the ceremonies surrounding death.

A further two items "A Touching Place" and "Be Still and Know" have also been recorded by the Cathedral Singers and are represented in octavos in the GOD NEVER SLEEPS collection.

Further hymns, songs, and liturgical materials produced by John L. Bell and Graham Maule may be found in these books, published in Great Britain by Wild Goose Publications (The Iona Community), in North America by GIA Publications, Inc. of Chicago, and represented in Australia and New Zealand by Willow Publications of Sydney.